Dear Debra

You are more ~~better~~ special
than you realise and I
feel blessed that you're
my friend.

Lots of Love Nat
x
23.03.09

A friend is the person whose e-mail
you'll open when it's a bad hair day.

A friend is a person with
whom you dare to be yourself.

A friend forgives your foibles, rejoices in your triumphs, comforts you in sorrow.

M<small>Y WORLD IS MADE BY MY FRIENDS.</small>

A friend's writing on
an envelope lifts the heart
on the rainiest morning.

Every good thing is better if you can share it with a friend.

FRIENDSHIP IS WHAT SHOWS US THAT WE ARE NOT ALONE IN ANY JOY OR ANY SORROW.

Friends have come to an agreement. You put up with my idiosyncrasies. I'll put up with yours!

Friends put the entire world to rights over a cup of tea and a scrumptious home-baked pie.

Only a friend can tell you that your hair is a preposterous red or that you're wearing odd shoes.

A friend is a bridge into a wider world. We see through their eyes as well as through our own.

A friend is the person to whom you'll open the door when nobody else will do.

A really good friend helps you face the truth
and stays beside you, whatever comes.

To have even one good friend
is to keep the darkness at bay.

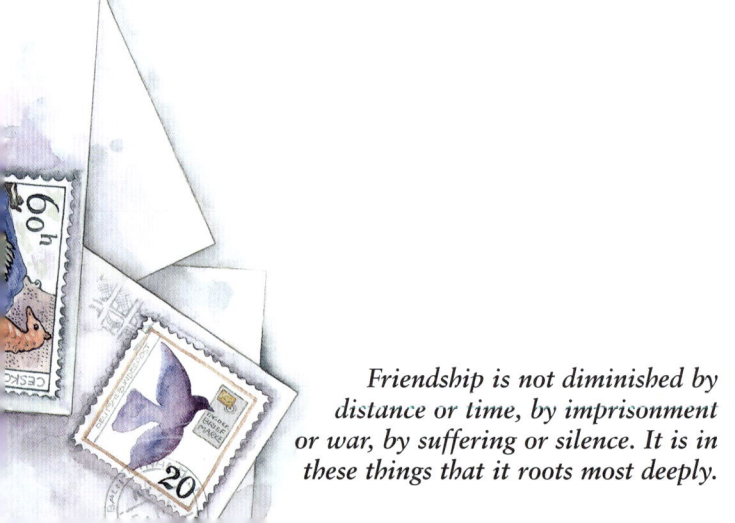

Friendship is not diminished by distance or time, by imprisonment or war, by suffering or silence. It is in these things that it roots most deeply.

Friendships are glued
together with little kindnesses.

It is our friends who
help us through our disillusions.

We need a friend's care and kindness – and find
delight in discovering they need us too.

A friend is there for you
when things go wrong
– and never says I told you so.

OLD FRIENDS STAY THE SAME AGE FOREVER.

It is the small, simple gestures that make life bearable. A smile, a touch, a kindness, a concern.

The world is so wide and each of us so small – yet bound by friendship we are giants.

FRIENDSHIP CAN MAKE THE UNBEARABLE
BEARABLE.

A friend, by a phone call, a popping-in, a small unexpected surprise, puts a little jam on the day's bread and butter.

A friend believes in you
when no one else does.

Friends make it possible to
live in a cruel world.

Love is blind;
friendship quietly closes its eyes.

Friends don't egg you on to buy things. They say very firmly "It doesn't suit you".

FRIENDSHIPS LINK AND LOOP AND
INTERWEAVE UNTIL THEY MESH THE WORLD.

How fortunate I am to have a friend like you. Someone to laugh with, share secrets, a reassurance in the darkest times.

There are times when we most need friends. Ready to do anything or go anywhere. Thank you for doing, being, just that.

There is such a difference
between being a little daft
all on your own – and being
a little daft together.

Thank you for the
stupendous, the outrageous
surprises that light up
the dull days.

Thank you for making me laugh when I'd almost forgotten how to.

You text me on my mobile
– and make me feel I'm necessary
to someone.

Other people are
sympathetic, concerned, kind
– but never there.
You are – whenever I
most need you.

Thank you for making me feel life is worth having – whatever happens.

You make me forget the dreary days –
and make the bright ones magical.

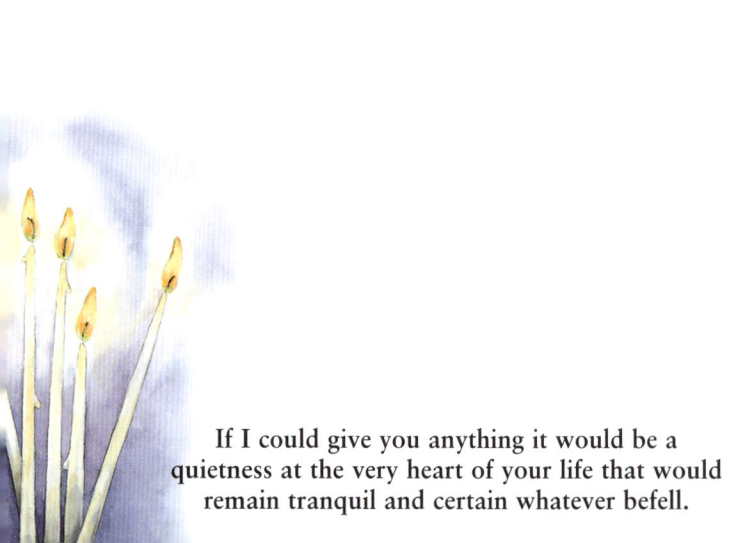

If I could give you anything it would be a
quietness at the very heart of your life that would
remain tranquil and certain whatever befell.

May the coming years bring you new hopes, new beginnings, new adventures, new discoveries.

LET ME THANK YOU FOR ALL THE TIMES THAT I
FORGOT TO THANK YOU — TAKING YOUR LOVE AND
FORGIVENESS FOR GRANTED.

I suppose I could have struggled through without you. But thank heavens I didn't have to.

THANK YOU FOR SIMPLY BEING YOU – CONSTANT IN
FRIENDSHIP, UNFAILING IN KINDNESS.

I wish you discoveries and marvels. I wish you
joy and peace and deep contentment. And always,
always, love.

Text by Pam Brown • Illustrated by Juliette Clarke • Created by Helen Exley

Published simultaneously in 2004 by Exley Publications Ltd in Great Britain,
and Exley Publications LLC in the USA. Copyright © Helen Exley 2004. Pam Brown,
J.R.C., Helen Exley, Marion C. Garretty, Charlotte Gray, Jane Swan, Mercia Tweedale: pub
lished with permission © Helen Exley 2004.

Selection and Arrangement copyright © Helen Exley 2004

12 11 10 9 8 7 6 5 4

ISBN 1-86187-577-0
A copy of the CIP data is available from the British Library. All rights reserved. No part of this publication may
be reproduced in any form. Printed in China.

What is a Helen Exley Giftbook?

Helen Exley Giftbooks cover the most powerful of all human relationships:
the bonds within families and between friends, and the theme of personal values.
No expense is spared in making sure that each book is as thoughtful and meaningful a
gift as it is possible to create: good to give, good to receive. You have the result in your
hands. If you have loved it – tell others! There is no power on earth like the word-of-
mouth recommendation of friends.

Other Helen Exley Giftbooks:

To a very special Friend

The Love Between Friends

Words on the power of Friendship

A Little Book for a Friend

In Praise and Celebration of Friends

A Friend...

Thank Heavens for Friends

The notebooks in this series of twelve are complemented by a range of mini gifts of themed magnets, photo frames, candles and gift bags.

Notebook for a very special grandma

Notebook for a very special mother

New Baby Notebook

Notebook for a very special sister

Wedding Notebook.

and many more...

Exley Publications Ltd, 16 Chalk Hill, Watford, Herts WD19 4BG, UK.
Exley Publications LLC, 185 Main Street, Spencer, MA 01562, USA.
www.helenexleygiftbooks.com